How To Negotiate a Behavioral Contract

SECOND EDITION

R. Vance Hall
and
Marilyn L. Hall

How To Manage Behavior Series

R. Vance Hall
and
Marilyn L. Hall
Series Editors

pro·ed
An International Publisher
8700 Shoal Creek Boulevard
Austin, Texas 78757-6897
800/897-3202 Fax 800/397-7633
Order online at http://www.proedinc.com

© 1998 by PRO-ED, Inc.
8700 Shoal Creek Boulevard
Austin, Texas 78757-6897
www.proedinc.com

Library of Congress Cataloging-in-Publication Data

Hall, R. Vance (Robert Vance), 1928–
    How to negotiate a behavioral contract / R. Vance Hall, Marilyn L. Hall.—2nd ed.
      p.   cm.—(How to manage behavior series)
    Includes bibliographical references.
    ISBN 0-89079-765-X (alk. paper)
    1. Behavior modification.   2. Learning contracts.   I. Hall, Marilyn C. II. Title. III. Series
LB1060.2.H345   1998
371.39'3—dc21   97-45685
                                                    CIP

This book is designed in Palatino and Frutiger.

Printed in the United States of America

6 7 8 9 10   09 08

Contents

Preface to Series

The first edition of the *How To Manage Behavior Series* was launched some 15 years ago in response to a perceived need for teaching aids that could be used by therapists and trainers. The widespread demand for the series has demonstrated the need by therapists and trainers for nontechnical materials for training and treatment aids for parents, teachers, and students. Publication of this revised series includes many updated titles of the original series. In addition, several new titles have been added, largely in response to therapists and trainers who have used the series. A few titles of the original series that proved to be in less demand have been replaced. We hope the new titles will increase the usefulness of the series.

The editors are indebted to Steven Mathews, Vice President of PRO-ED, who was instrumental in the production of the revised series, as was Robert K. Hoyt, Jr. of H & H Enterprises in producing the original version.

These books are designed to teach practitioners, including parents, specific behavioral procedures to use in managing the behaviors of children, students, and other persons whose behavior may be creating disruption or interference at home, at school, or on the job. The books are nontechnical, step-by-step instructional manuals that define the procedure, provide numerous examples, and allow the reader to make oral or written responses.

The exercises in these books are designed to be used under the direction of someone (usually a professional) with a background in the behavioral principles and procedures on which the techniques are based.

The booklets in the series are similar in format but are flexible enough to be adapted to a number of different teaching situations and training environments.

As always, we invite your comments, suggestions, and questions. We are always happy to hear of your successes in changing your own behaviors and the behaviors of other persons to make your lives more pleasant, productive, and purposeful.

R. Vance Hall &
Marilyn L. Hall,
Series Editors

How To Manage Behavior Series

How To Maintain Behavior

How To Motivate Others Through Feedback

How To Negotiate a Behavioral Contract

How To Select Reinforcers

How To Teach Social Skills

How To Teach Through Modeling and Imitation

How To Use Group Contingencies

How To Use Planned Ignoring

How To Use Prompts To Initiate Behavior

How To Use Response Cost

How To Use Systematic Attention and Approval

How To Use Time-Out

Introduction

This manual is for parents, teachers, childcare workers, counselors, staff members of institutions for individuals who are mentally ill or retarded, employers, marital partners, and others who may want to negotiate behavioral contracts. It is designed to be used under the supervision of a counselor or other professional person familiar with the proper use of behavioral contracts. The format enables the instructor to review the fill-in information provided by the reader and to use that feedback to assure the reader's proper understanding and use of behavioral contracts.

All of us use some kind of behavioral contracting each day, wittingly or unwittingly, and some form of negotiation, in our interactions with other persons. Sometimes those informal arrangements work, and sometimes they do not. With this booklet, the time for trial and error and hoping for the best is past. Using properly negotiated contracts, as explained in this manual, both parties have a chance to have a say and an opportunity to suggest alternate behaviors or rewards. If the negotiation is carried out in good faith, both parties will feel positive about signing the contract, know that it is fair, and have an interest in seeing that the contract brings about the desired changes in the behaviors of everyone involved.

Anyone who wants to change someone else's behavior, and is willing to give up something in return, will be able to use this manual to draw up a contract to ensure that the behaviors he or she wishes to change will be clearly defined and that the rewards for those behaviors (including how the rewards will be delivered) are spelled out for everyone so there is no misunderstanding and so the contract benefits everyone who is a party to it.

Behavioral contracts have been used informally in many situations for a long time. Recently they have been used in a more structured systematic manner in home, work, and educational settings to change various behaviors.

Behavioral contracts are particularly useful with adolescents. Parents of teenagers have found they can use behavioral contracts in cases where other procedures such as planned ignoring and time-out have been ineffective. As is pointed out in *How To Use Time-Out*, (Hall & Hall, 1998d), time-out is of limited

R. Vance Hall, PhD, is Senior Scientist Emeritus of The Bureau of Child Research and Professor Emeritus of Human Development and Family Life and Special Education at the University of Kansas. He was a pioneer in carrying out behavioral research in classrooms and in homes. Marilyn L. Hall, EdD, taught and carried out research in regular and special public school classrooms. While at the University of Kansas, she developed programs for training parents to use systematic behavior change procedures and was a successful behavior therapist specializing in child management and marriage relationships.

usefulness for persons over 12 years old. Behavioral contracts, however, are especially useful for older youths and adults.

Properly implemented, behavioral contracting is a procedure that avoids ethical pitfalls sometimes associated with the use of powerful behavior change procedures. If properly negotiated, a behavioral contract provides the informed consent of the other person and results in an improved situation for all concerned. Another advantage of the proper use of behavioral contracts is that they can begin in a situation in which a person's behavior is out of control, provide external control, and finally lead to self-control. Self-control should be the ultimate goal of any person who uses behavioral contracting. An ideal program starts with a behavior that is not under control, and is often a source of disharmony and fighting. The first stage to overcome is the one in which the person initiating the contract imposes a certain amount of external control (through a manager's role) in arriving at a contract. Even here, however, the other person has some input if the contract is properly negotiated. Over time, the contract should shift to one in which there is joint control—that is, control or responsibility equally shared by both parties. The final stages are where the person begins to manage his or her own behavior and the contract is faded, and natural and social reinforcers maintain the behavior. If this happens, the person has control of both the behavior that was formerly a problem and the consequences that control the new behavior.

What Is a Behavioral Contract?

It is easiest and most natural to arrange contingencies and deliver consequences in an informal manner. In most interactions in the home, at school, in the community, or at work, you do not need to stop and think, "Now it is time to reinforce" or "I had better reward that behavior." The delivery of some reinforcement becomes a habit. However, there are times when an informal approach to providing rewards and other consequences of behavior is not effective. If you become particularly concerned about a specific behavior and your informal efforts to bring about an improved situation fail, it may become necessary to set up a structured contingency system. This may be true even if you have tried other management techniques.

A structured contingency system helps arrange your thinking so the behaviors you wish to change are clearly defined and the rewards for those behaviors (including when and how rewards will be delivered) are spelled out for everyone involved.

A behavioral contract is an agreement between two or more persons (parent and child, husband and wife, employer and employee, teacher and student) that lists specific behaviors the parties will perform and the consequences that will result. Behavior contracts, if properly negotiated, include clearly specified behaviors and rewards. The purpose of the contract is to systematically arrange for reinforcers to be exchanged by two or more individuals to reach a desired goal. Contracts need not be long and elaborate. The simpler the better. In reality, a behavioral contract is a formal statement of what has been labeled "Grandma's Law": Grandma used to say, "When you say please (eat your spinach, etc.), then you may have a cookie (go out to play, etc.)." Basically, Grandma's Law states that first you do something, then you get what you want.

Have you ever used Grandma's Law?

When and how? _____

_____

_____

_____

_____

Examples of Behavioral Contracts in Use

At Home

Mrs. Alison became increasingly aggravated by her 16-year-old son, Kyle, because his bedroom always seemed to look like a disaster area. She had found it increasingly difficult to get him to make his bed, and to keep clean clothes put away in closets and drawers and dirty clothes in the clothes hamper. Kyle, on the other hand, resented his mother's constant nagging and reluctance to let him use the family car. Their conflicts had resulted in several shouting matches.

Finally, in desperation, Mrs. Alison negotiated a written agreement with Kyle that said if he made his bed Sunday through Friday and kept his clothes in their proper places, she would agree not to nag him more than two times a week and he could have the use of the car on Friday or Saturday evening or on Sunday afternoon. After that, both were more satisfied and their shouting matches became much less frequent. Mrs. Alison no longer felt the need to nag, and Kyle was pleased to know that he could count on using the car on weekends.

At School

Sarah Cook had always found it difficult to turn in her assignments on time and as a result had never been a very good math student. However, when she was assigned to Mr. Jones' eighth-grade algebra class, she found that he had a system under which all of the students signed an agreement that if everyone in the class handed in four out of five completed homework assignments each week, the class would get to play favorite records and talk during the last 20 minutes of class each Friday. From then on Sarah managed to complete almost every assignment and for the first time she began to get good grades in math. Mr. Jones was pleased because Sarah and her classmates were making good progress in Algebra, and even he looked forward to the break the students earned each Friday.

At Work

Mr. Overmann had tried without success to get his waitresses to consistently suggest to customers that they order wine with their meals. Finally, he prepared a contract in which each waitress promised to ask all adult customers to buy wine and he promised to pay each of them a bonus if wine sales increased 25% and a bigger bonus if they increased 50%. As a result wine sales increased 100% almost immediately.

In Marriage

John and Beth Allen sought marriage counseling because they had become disenchanted with each other. John thought Beth was too undisciplined about regular meal times, and Beth thought John was too busy to pursue any social life with her. At the suggestion of their marriage counselor, they signed a series of contracts. One specified that if Beth had dinner on the table each evening between 6:00 and 6:15 P.M. Beth could choose for them to go out to dinner, go to a show, or entertain or visit friends on either Friday or Saturday evening. After they learned to negotiate their own behavioral contracts, either written or informal, both reported their marriage much improved and they terminated the counseling sessions.

The examples above illustrate typical situations in which written behavioral contracts (sometimes called contingency contracts) are used. Contracts can be used as alternatives to shouting, arguing, and fighting. Behavioral contracts specify who is to engage in what behaviors, what the consequences will be, and who will provide the consequences. In each case above, all parties who signed the contracts received something.

Describe a behavioral contract and what it does.

What it is: _____

_____

_____

_____

_____

What it does: _____

_____

_____

_____

You are on target if you said a behavioral contract is a written agreement between two or more persons that tells what behaviors will be performed and what rewards or consequences will result. It formalizes an exchange of behaviors and reinforcers.

Now let us look more closely at what is involved in writing a good behavioral contract.

Basic Rules for Making Contracts

Once we have defined and given some examples of behavioral contracts, it may appear that making a contract is a simple procedure. Nevertheless, it is not always easy to make a good contract. However, now that you have an idea about what they are and what they do, you are ready to learn the rules to be followed to write an effective contract.

▶ Rule 1: Select behaviors that are socially and educationally important.

Whatever behaviors or tasks are selected should be of importance or concern to all parties involved. Behavioral contracts require considerable work to write, monitor, and carry out. They must be worth the effort.

There are a number of ways to go about selecting an important behavior. Sometimes behaviors become of such concern that we have little trouble choosing them. In other cases, choosing a behavior may require more thought. If there are a number of behaviors of concern, it may be necessary to list several tasks or behaviors before choosing one to change.

Step 1. One way to choose a behavior is to meet with the person or persons involved and try to list the behaviors you both feel are important. Arrange a family or staff meeting and ask the persons involved to list behaviors of concern. Have the persons first list behaviors they do well. For example, Mrs. Alison began working with her son, Kyle, by showing him a list of things she had jotted down that Kyle did to her satisfaction.

Things Kyle does well:

1. Mows the lawn every week (shovels the walk in winter)

2. Has a neat personal appearance

3. Gets good grades in school

4. Treats his younger brother, Phil, very well

5. Carries out the trash without griping

6. Drives safely

7. Comes home on time or calls

8. Earns own spending money

They then made a list for Mrs. Alison.

Things mother does well:

1. Gets meals on time

2. Washes and irons the clothes

3. Supports the family by working

4. Makes super spaghetti

5. Cleans the house and keeps it neat

6. Buys the gas for the car

7. Takes Phil to soccer practice

8. Waters the house plants

9. Goes to see Kyle play on the soccer team

10. Does the grocery shopping (Kyle sometimes helps)

Step 2. Making these lists got things off on a positive note. Next they made lists of things they might do better.

Things Kyle could do to improve:

1. Make bed every day

2. Help more with the dishes

3. Put clean clothes in drawers and closets

4. Put dirty clothes in clothes hamper

5. Keep school books out of the living room

6. Don't leave gas tank empty when using the car

7. Fix supper when mother gets home late

8. Not play stereo so loud after supper

Things mother could do to improve:

1. Not nag about little things so much

2. Show more appreciation for the things Kyle does do right

3. <u>Quit smoking</u>

4. <u>Get more exercise</u>

5. <u>Make more pies (banana cream)</u>

6. <u>Clean hair out of shower drain</u>

In making lists, be specific. List specific tasks to do or not do. The following are examples of specific statements (right) and vague statements (wrong).

Right	Wrong
Comes home on time or calls	Is not prompt
Puts clean clothes in drawers or closet	Is messy

In the list they made for Mrs. Alison, they might have written, "Walk and jog 2 miles 3 times a week" rather than "Get more exercise."

If you have a person in mind with whom you would like to negotiate a behavioral contract, make a list of some things that person does well. (Remember to be specific.)

Things Done Well

1. _____

2. _____

3. _____

4. _____

5. _____

6. _____

Now make a list of behaviors you would like to see improved. (Write the behavior you do want, not the behavior you do not want.)

(continues)

Things To Improve

1. _____

2. _____

3. _____

4. _____

5. _____

6. _____

The following are questions you can ask yourself that will help you decide if the behaviors are important.

If the person did it, would it really make things better?
Is it something the person can do?
Is this the logical person to do it?

If you plan to exchange behaviors with another person, consider making a list for yourself.

Things I Do Well

1. _____

2. _____

3. _____

4. _____

5. _____

6. _____

Things I Could or Should Do Better

1. _____

2. _____

(continues)

3. _____

4. _____

5. _____

6. _____

▶ **Rule 2: Include only one or a few closely related target behaviors.**

From the list above, select one target behavior for the person with whom you want to set up a contract.

Write the target behavior you have selected here: _____

_____

▶ **Rule 3: Make a list of possible rewards (reinforcers) that are meaningful and fair.**

Just as it is sometimes necessary to list target behaviors for contracts, it is also necessary to list potential rewards. It is essential to ask the other person to help compile the list; otherwise, you may choose a reward that is inappropriate.

In Kyle's case, the list he and his mother made included the following rewards:

1. Listening to CDs on the stereo

2. Going to movies

3. Driving the car

4. Having a party

5. Staying out late

6. Money

7. _Going to a professional sporting event_ _____

8. _Praise rather than nagging from mother_ _____

One office manager made the following list of potential rewards available for secretaries working under his supervision:

1. Early lunch break
2. Early coffee break
3. Free coffee
4. Selection of preferred computer tasks
5. Selection of preferred work station
6. Employee of the month award
7. Letter of commendation
8. Increase in salary
9. Earned time off

There are many consequences you can consider providing for the behaviors you wish to change. They can be toys, books, clothes, and money. They can be privileges and activities, such as going to a movie or going out to eat. They can be social interactions, such as having time alone with parent or, in the case of household partners, having 10 minutes of time to talk about a subject of personal concern. In an office, they can include privileges, recognition, and material rewards. If you have trouble finding a reward that works, you may wish to consult _How To Select Reinforcers_ (Hall & Hall, 1998a).

Make a list of potential rewards (reinforcers) for the person with whom you plan to negotiate a contract.

1. _____

2. _____

3. _____

4. _____

5. _____

(continues)

6. _____

7. _____

▶ **Rule 4: Have the contract written and signed.**

Verbal contracts that are not specific and signed are open to misunderstanding and misinterpretation.

▶ **Rule 5: Have the contract written in positive terms.**

State the desired behavior, not the behavior you do not want. For example, "Payton will list all sales contacts before leaving the office" is better than "If Payton doesn't file all sales contacts before leaving the office . . ." or "Casey will get a B or above in science" is better than "If Casey doesn't make at least a B . . . ."

In other words, put the contract in the form of Grandma's Law. When the desired behavior is observed, then the reinforcement is given.

Some of the examples below state a behavior in positive terms. If you think they are positive, write OK on the line below each of them. If they are too negative, rewrite them.

EXAMPLE: Jerry won't empty the trash.

Jerry will empty the trash each day by 6:30 P.M.

1. If Jana doesn't do her homework by 9:00 P.M. . . .

   _____

2. Mr. Mirman will answer the telephone before it rings four times.

   _____

3. Dana must stop hitting his classmates and calling them names.

   _____

(continues)

4. Sam will mow the lawn by 4:30 P.M. each Saturday.

_____

5. Kisha will quit cutting into the lunch line.

_____

You have the idea if you said Statements 2 and 4 were okay and rewrote the others in more positive terms.

▶ **Rule 6: Make contracts specific regarding the behavior and the consequences.**

The following information should be included.

Behavior	Consequence
Who (person performing the behavior)	Who (person providing the consequence)
What (specific behavior)	What (the consequence will be)
When (it will occur)	When (the consequence will occur)
How much (include all expectations)	How much (how long it will last, exceptions, alternate consequence, if needed)

List the specifics you might include in a contract to change a behavior in someone you know.

Behavior	Consequence
Who _____	Who _____
What_____	What_____
When _____	When _____
How much _____	How much _____

▶ **Rule 7: Contracts should have a definite beginning and end.**

Most contracts begin when they are signed and end at a time stated in the contract. Contracts can either be renegotiated or faded out at the end of the contract period. Note that in the sample contracts that follow a definite beginning and end are provided.

The following contract was negotiated by Mr. Jones with Sarah and the members of her algebra class.

CONTRACT	
Behavior	**Consequence**
Who: Members of 5th period algebra class	Who: Mr. Jones
What: Completing homework assignment	What: Class members can play records, talk, chew gum
When: Must be handed in at beginning of next day's algebra period	When: Friday afternoons from 2:35–2:55 P.M. through the semester
How much: All class members must hand in 4 out of 5 completed assignments	How much: As freely as desired as long as it doesn't disrupt other classes (no scuffling, running, etc.)
Signed _____(see below)_____ Date _Sept. 8_	Signed _____Gerald Jones_____ Date _Sept. 8_

	Tally
Sarah Cook	ⅢⅡ
Jane Anderson	ⅢⅡ
Bill Bery	ⅢⅡ
John Carson	ⅢⅡ
Susie Shaw	|||
Clyde Ralston	ⅢⅡ

This classroom contract was signed by Mr. Jones and all the members of his eighth-grade algebra class. It was posted on the bulletin board above a box just inside the classroom door. It was designed so a new tagboard strip could be pinned to it each week next to each student's signature. Each day a student was assigned to check to see if homework assignments were handed in. A tally was recorded on the strip if the pupil had attempted to solve all the assigned problems. This system allowed one contract to serve for an entire semester and also provided a record of fulfillment of the behavior.

The following is one in a series of contracts negotiated between John and Beth with the help of their marriage counselor. Note that a place to keep track of the behaviors was provided.

CONTRACT	
Behavior	**Consequence**
Who: I, Beth Allen	Who: I, John Allen
What: Will let John have a beer and the paper without disturbance	What: Will arrive home from work no later than 5:15 P.M. and will converse with Beth during dinner
When: From the time he arrives home until supper at 6:00–6:15 P.M.	When: Every working day unless arranged for in advance
How much: Every working day through January unless we go out	How much: Will sit at the table, eat and talk for at least 30 minutes
Signed ___Beth Allen___ Date __Jan. 4__	Signed ___John Allen___ Date __Jan. 4__

Mon	Tues	Wed	Thur	Fri

Mon	Tues	Wed	Thur	Fri

The following contract was negotiated between a father, Jim Finley, and his son, Pat.

CONTRACT	
Behavior	**Consequence**

Behavior

Who: _Pat Finley_

What: _Work on homework for 1 hour_

When: _Before any TV and prior to 10:00 P.M., Sun through Thurs_

How much: _Time must be actively engaged in reading, writing, or solving problems_

Signed _____Pat Finley_____ Date _Oct. 14_

Consequence

Who: _Jim Finley_

What: _TV watching and pay for report card grades_

When: _After one hour of homework_

How much: _As much TV as he wants, $5 for a C, $10 for a B and $20 for an A_

Signed _____J. T. Finley_____ Date _Oct. 14_

Minutes of Study

	Sun	Mon	Tues	Wed	Thur
Oct 15	60	65	60	72	64
Oct 22	~~22~~	71	68	60	64
Oct 29	122	61	63	~~48~~	62

	Sun	Mon	Tues	Wed	Thur
Nov 5	69	71			
Nov 12			Grades Out		

Grades

Math _____ English _____ Science _____

PE _____ Drama _____ Shop _____

▶ **Rule 8: Provide frequent reinforcement that immediately follows the behavior.**

Long-term contracts that allow long delays between the behavior and rewards are not likely to succeed. This is especially true with young children. A contract that provides big rewards earned after a long period of time will be more successful if there are smaller intermediate rewards along the way. Pat Finley's father followed this rule when he allowed Pat to watch television as a daily reward for Pat's studying. The longer term reinforcement came as an opportunity to earn pay for improved report card grades. One parent followed this technique by allowing his son to earn a bicycle piece by piece rather than having him wait until he had earned the entire bike. In this way the son accumulated tangible evidence that he was making progress. Earning the various bicycle parts helped bridge the time between when he began earning the parts until he had a complete bike.

Because it is important to provide frequent and immediate reinforcement in establishing behavior, it is difficult for some persons to keep doing the behavior long enough to meet the terms of the contract and receive a reward. If that happens, you should renegotiate the contract, setting new standards the person can meet. After he or she experiences success, you can often change back to the original terms. If your first contract is unsuccessful, renegotiate.

▶ Rule 9: Provide attention and approval for progress toward fulfilling the contract.

One thing you can do to help bridge the gap, especially for young persons, is to provide lots of praise and approval for their efforts. Encourage them for any improvement and tell them you know they are going to earn the reward. Such social reinforcement can be very effective in bridging the time between doing the behavior and receiving the reward. Remember, you want the contract to succeed. Do whatever you can to make it happen. Praise frequently paired with success and other reinforcers will maintain a great deal of behavior, and the contracting will become less necessary.

In the spaces below, list some potential rewards a person could be given soon after he or she fulfills a contract by performing a behavior.

1. _____

2. _____

3. _____

▶ **Rule 10: A good contract should ensure success.**

A contract should provide frequent reinforcement and require behavior the person can reasonably perform. One goal of the contract should be to require an improvement in behavior that is noticeable and important, but that behavior should be a goal the person can most likely reach. After the person has successfully completed one contract, new contracts can be negotiated for higher goals.

For example, one repair shop employer (whose workers were completing only 38% of repair jobs on time) negotiated a contract that resulted in repairs being completed 55% on time. Subsequent contracts increased jobs completed on time to 75% and finally to 95%.

Consider using shaping to make sure your contract is successful (see Panyan, 1980). Settle first for modest improvement (or improvement in one area), and then seek further gains in subsequent contracts.

Describe how much behavior change you think is reasonable for the first step of your contract.

Do you think the person can reach that goal successfully?   Yes ☐   No ☐

▶ **Rule 11: Contracts should be negotiated and should be fair to both parties.**

Negotiation should be a part of every behavioral contract activity. In fact, a board game called Negotiation has been designed to help parents and teenagers learn to negotiate successful contracts (Campbell, 1981). For a contract to be successful, the person who will perform the behavior must feel that he or she is getting a worthwhile reward for what he or she is to do. On the other hand, the person providing the consequence must feel that the behavior is important enough so that he or she can willingly and honestly provide the reward if the behavior is performed. This can usually be assured if both parties are involved in selecting the behaviors and consequences. If a parent, teacher, or employer imposes a contract on a person, it may fail because one person cannot always arbitrarily decide on rewards that are fair in relation to the behavior required.

In a negotiated contract, both parties have a chance to suggest alternate behaviors or rewards. If the negotiation is carried out in good faith, both will feel positive about signing a contract they feel is fair.

Select a fair reward for each of the behaviors listed. Consider the following potential reinforcers: $100, watch TV for an hour, $10 a week raise in pay, use of the car for one night a week, $20 weekly allowance, a letter of commendation.

Behavior	Suggested Reward
a. Nine-year-old Bill will write each spelling word correctly three times Monday through Thursday after supper.	_____
b. Carmen Stem will type and return 9 of 10 letters to Mr. Delgardi within 2 hours from April 1 to May 15.	_____
c. Tad Iown will mail in his book manuscript by September 1.	_____
d. Seventeen-year-old Bob Hight will mow the lawn, wash the car, and sweep the patio every Saturday morning (by 12:00 P.M.).	_____

It would depend on the persons involved, but we chose the following rewards: a. TV, b. $10 a week raise, c. $100, d. use of the car. Did you agree?

▶ **Rule 12: Contracts should allow for renegotiation.**

Contracts may be renegotiated for the following reasons:

1. The contract was completed or the time period covered by the contract is ended.

2. A step toward the desired behavior has been reached and you are ready to move on to the next step.

3. The contract is not working.

   In cases in which the contract has been fulfilled and the behavior has been rewarded, you will need to consider whether a new contract is needed. It is possible that both parties will want to continue the same contract for a new period or perhaps revise it only slightly to include added behaviors for similar or new rewards. If at any time during the contract it becomes clear that the contract is not working, it is necessary to renegotiate. This may mean that the kind or amount of behavior requirements needs to be changed or that the consequences for the behavior needs to be adjusted. It is better to renegotiate a contract than to let it flounder and fail.

▶ **Rule 13: Keep a record of performance on the contracted behavior.**

It is extremely important that a record be kept of the behavior required to fulfill the contract. This is usually easy to accomplish if the behavior has been clearly specified.

It is a good idea to keep the record right on the contract. The contract thus becomes a document that spells out the behavior and tells how well the person is carrying out his or her part.

Although the kind of record depends on the behavior, the record is usually a form where success in performing the behavior is noted every time it happens. For example, in the following contract between a mother and her daughter, space was provided for checking whether or not the daughter finished doing the dishes within 30 minutes after the last person got up from the supper table.

CONTRACT	
Behavior	**Consequence**
Who: Alice Smith	Who: Betsy Smith
What: Wash, dry, put away dishes, wash table, clean sink	What: Alice will be allowed to read in bed
When: Within 30 min after the last person leaves the table	When: After her regular lights-out time of 9:00 P.M.
How much: After every evening meal and Sunday dinner for 1 month	How much: 15 min Sun. through Thurs., 30 min Fri. & Sat. on days she fulfills contract
Signed ___Alice Smith___ Date __Feb. 3__	Signed ___Betsy Smith___ Date __Feb. 3__

Sun	Mon	Tues	Wed	Thur	Fri	Sat
28	34 ✔	27	25	26	49 ✔	24
25	20	19	18	20	17	22
30	18	19	15	18	22	29
17	18	21	18	19		

This contract was taped to the refrigerator door (a good place to post contracts). Alice used the timer on the kitchen stove to time herself. It was set to go off 30 minutes after the last person left the table. It became a game to set it at the exact moment the last person arose from his or her chair and for Alice to begin. Alice recorded the time that had elapsed on the timer when she had put away the last dish and had wiped off the table and the kitchen sink. As can be seen by the record, except for two nights, she earned a longer reading time each night and by the end of the month was usually finished in 20 minutes or less. Incidentally, after the month was over and the contract was faded, Alice continued to do the dishes quickly (she almost always timed herself) and her parents let her keep her extended reading privileges.

In the following contract, under the signatures, devise a form for recording for 1 month John's behaviors and the times he gets to use the car.

CONTRACT	
Behavior	**Consequence**
Who: _John_	Who: _Dad_
What: _Will be in the house_	What: _Will let John use the car_
When: _by 11 P.M. Sun through Thurs, 1:00 P.M. Fri & Sat_	When: _On weekend night or afternoon_
How much: _One exception per week by prior agreement with Dad_	How much: _Once per week not counting errands for Dad or Mom_
Signed _John Boi_ Date _May 2_	Signed _Bill Boi_ Date _May 2_

If a contract is written so the behavior needs to be checked only once (at the end of the contract), record keeping is no problem. In some cases records are already available (e.g., absentee records in most places of employment). It may still be a good idea to keep a visual record. In the case below, office records were available of Sally Slick's sales, but she and her sales manager decided to keep a chart of her sales. Progress is easier to follow if simple graphs are used.

CONTRACT	
Behavior	**Consequence**
Who: Salesperson, Sally Slick	Who: Sales manager, Rick Lewis
What: Will increase total sales	What: New 19" color TV
When: each month, Feb., March, & April	When: By May 3rd
How much: to $20,000 or more gross	How much: Choice of Zenith, Magnavox, or RCA
Signed Sally Slick Date July 28	Signed Rick Lewis Date July 28

Before Contract   After Contract

▶ **Rule 14: Fade out written contracts after new patterns of behavior and reinforcement have been established.**

A primary goal of behavioral contracting should be to eventually decrease the dependency on the contract and to maintain the newly established behaviors and reinforcers informally in the natural environment. This is one reason why it is usually best to contract to improve only one behavior at a time. After a behavior has been established and becomes habitual, it is maintained by praise or other naturally available consequences. A formal contract is then no longer necessary as long as the person continues to receive enough reinforcement to maintain the new behavior. As a matter of fact, once a behavior is established, it is more likely to continue if reinforcement is less frequent.

One way to fade out a contract is for both parties to agree informally that the behavior will continue and the persons will continue to receive certain privileges or other rewards without a formal accounting.

Then both parties are free to negotiate another contract for another behavior of concern. As the contracting parties become skilled at performing appropriate behavior and arranging for rewarding consequences, there is less and less necessity for formal structured arrangements. However, any time the parties find they are in conflict over performance, they may need to set up a new behavioral contract in order to avoid the arguing and fighting that often occurs when behavior is demanded and not rewarded.

How will you fade out a contract you are planning to negotiate?

_____

_____

_____

Behavioral Contract Forms

Behavioral contracts have been written in many forms. The form on the following page is designed to clearly state the specific behaviors and consequences that make up the contract. The language of the contract should be straightforward and simple so the terms are clear to everyone concerned.

The following form may be copied and used to create behavioral contracts. You may modify this form or use it as a model for making your own form.

CONTRACT	
Behavior	**Consequence**
Who: _____	Who: _____
_____	_____
What: _____	What: _____
_____	_____
When: _____	When: _____
_____	_____
How much: _____	How much: _____
_____	_____
_____	_____
_____	_____
Signed _____ Date _____	Signed _____ Date _____

You have learned what should be entered in the blanks labeled Who, What, and When. The How Much blank is used for necessary details and to eliminate loopholes and misunderstandings. Every contract should be signed by all parties. The space at the bottom of the contract is for keeping a record of performance. Additional space on another piece of paper, a calendar, or another form may be used if necessary.

Although they usually require the person to have some level of reading skill, contracts can be negotiated with very young children and persons unable to read, in which cases pictures or symbols are used instead of writing. The following is an example of such a contract between a 43-year-old institutionalized adult with mental retardation (Bill) and his supervisor, Mr. James.

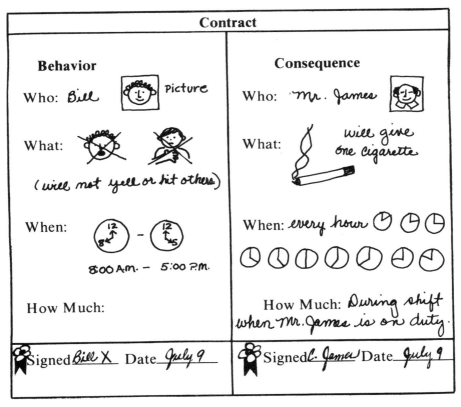

Some parents have made similar picture contracts with children as young as 3 years old. One parent used pictures to get her 4-year-old who is hearing impaired to remain in bed all night using a "Snoopy" blanket as a reward. She then negotiated a contract to get him to wear his hearing aid, using a pair of tennis shoes as a reward.

Make a picture contract for a child or an adult who is disabled.

CONTRACT	
Behavior	**Consequence**
Who:	Who:
What:	What:
When:	When:
How much:	How much:
Signed _____ Date _____	Signed _____ Date _____

Negotiating Your Own Contract

By now you should have a good grasp of the rules for negotiating a contract. Practice what you have learned by copying the blank contract form on page 24 and following the steps below in filling out a contract. If you have problems, go back and review the preceding rules and exercises.

Step 1. Sit down with the person and tell him or her you would like to negotiate a behavioral contract.

Explain that a behavioral contract is a written agreement that states what behaviors the two of you will perform and what rewards you will each receive for the behaviors. You may wish to state specifically which behaviors you want the person to perform, or you may wish to go through the exercise of having the person help you list several behaviors of concern from which to select a target behavior.

Step 2. Discuss with the person what reward or consequence you will provide if he or she performs the behavior.

You may wish to list or suggest several consequences or ask the person to suggest his or her own consequence. Remember that the consequences should be fair. The one that is selected should be appropriate to the amount of behavior required by the contract. It should be one you are sure you can provide, and it should be one that can be given frequently and immediately after the behavior is performed.

Stop and Consider: Steps 1 and 2 constitute the negotiation process. In carrying them out, you must make certain both parties have an opportunity to suggest alternate behaviors and rewards. Before you go on to the next step, both of you should feel you have negotiated a good contract that is fair to both parties. If you have mutually agreed to the behaviors and the rewards, go on to Step 3.

Step 3. Now you should be ready to write the contract.

Fill in the person's name after "Who" (or glue on a picture if the person is a nonreader).

Step 4. Write in the behavior after "What." Be sure that the goal (a) is stated in positive terms and (b) is specific.

(continues)

Step 5. Fill in "When." Use exact times.

Step 6. Fill in "How Much." Be sure to include any exceptions or special conditions.

Step 7. Fill in your own name under "Who" on the other side of the contract.

Step 8. Under "What," fill in the reward you will provide (or behavior you will engage in if it is an exchange of behaviors).

Be sure the reward is stated in specific terms that are clearly understood by all.

Step 9. Under "When," write down when you will provide the reward agreed upon.

Step 10. Under "How Much," write down any further statement needed to clarify the conditions of the rewarding consequence.

Step 11. Discuss with the person how you will keep track of performance.

Make a form for keeping a record in the space provided at the bottom of the contract.

Step 12. Go over the contract once more with the person.

If both of you are satisfied that it is fair and complete, sign and date it. (It is usually fun and appropriate to finish this ceremony by shaking hands.)

Step 13. Post the contract in a mutually agreed upon place.

Public posting will remind you and the other person about the contract. If for some reason you or the other person wishes to keep it private, put it in a less conspicuous but accessible place.

Checking Up

As you begin the contract, you will want to follow its progress, as described.

▶ **Follow-Up Step 1.** Make sure the behavior record is kept current and that you carry out your part of the contract. Remember to provide feedback and praise when the person is performing satisfactorily. Be sure that your rewards are delivered on time.

▶ **Follow-Up Step 2.** If the contract is not working—that is, if you or the other person seems to be failing to keep up your part of the contract—renegotiate. Clear up any misunderstanding and correct any loopholes.

▶ **Follow-Up Step 3.** When the behavior becomes established, try fading the contract by mutual consent and consider other behaviors to contract for with the person.

Potential Problems

1. Contracts not negotiated in good faith. The most frequent problem in behavioral contracting occurs when one person imposes his or her will on another. Such contracts have not been negotiated in good faith. To help determine whether the contract is negotiated in good faith, ask the question, "Did this contract really cost me something?" If the answer is "Yes," it is probably a good contract. If you have asked the other person to change a behavior that will take some effort on his or her part, you should expect that you will also provide something that will cause some effort or inconvenience on your part. If you are willing to give the other person something he or she really wants in exchange for something you really want, you have negotiated in good faith and your contract is likely to be a winner.

2. Major problems may prevent you from starting small. If a major problem must be dealt with immediately, you may not have the luxury of choosing which problem behaviors to deal with first. In such cases, it may be impossible to postpone dealing with a behavior of major concern. Even so, you may be able to ensure success by making the first contracts for a relatively short period so the person is more likely to fulfill the contract and to receive the reward agreed upon. If this short contract succeeds, another can be negotiated for a subsequent time of equal or perhaps even greater length, but still dealing with a major problem behavior.

3. Parties sometimes disagree about whether a contract has been fulfilled. If this happens, it probably means the contract was not specific enough or it contained a loophole. If this is the case, you should compromise and then make certain that there is no misunderstanding or loophole in subsequent contracts. The more contracts you negotiate, the more skilled you become in avoiding loopholes and problems of interpretation.

4. When to renegotiate? A relatively short duration for initial contracts is a good idea because you will not have to wait too long before renegotiating if it is unsuccessful. However, if it becomes apparent to either party that a contract is not working, it is probably better to go over the contract to make certain it is

being interpreted correctly or to renegotiate it so it does work. In other words, sooner is probably better than later when it comes to renegotiation.

5. Should there be penalties for failing to fulfill a contract? The penalty for not fulfilling a contract is that the person who fails to fulfill does not get the reward. If the reward offered is meaningful and important to the person, losing it should be punishment enough. Some persons may need to experience not receiving an agreed-upon reward before they will begin fulfilling contracts. In future contracts, it may be necessary to make additional privileges contingent on the desired behavior. If you have been providing too many privileges outside the contract, it may be necessary to provide those privileges as a reward for the contracted behavior.

6. What if an impasse is reached? If you have attempted to negotiate a contract and you come to a point where the other person is unwilling to trade a behavior for what you are willing to offer, ask yourself, "Am I being unreasonable or unfair in what I am willing to offer in this contract? Am I asking too much?" If your answer is "Yes" to either of these questions, go back to the bargaining table and try again. If the answer is "No," perhaps you can consider negotiating for an alternate behavior in the direction of the behavior you previously targeted.

Another alternative is to seek counseling with someone skilled in behavioral procedures. Such a person can help you and the other person overcome the impasse in your negotiations. When impasses occur, you have little to lose in seeking professional assistance.

Where To From Here?

If you have read this book and carried out the exercises, received feedback on your responses from an instructor, and negotiated a contract, you should have a good grasp of how to negotiate a behavioral contract. Behavioral contracting is like any other skill: The more you practice, the better you become. Persons who become skilled at negotiating formal written contracts also become more skilled in providing rewarding consequences for behavior in a more informal way. Such persons are known as good behavior managers. If one of your goals is to become better skilled at managing behavior, we hope the procedures in this book are useful in helping you to reach that goal. Good luck in all your future negotiations.

References and Further Reading

Axelrod, S. (1983). *Behavior modification for the classroom teacher.* New York: McGraw-Hill.

Bristol, M. M., & Sloane, H. N., Jr. (1974). Effects of contingency contracting on study rate and test performance. *Journal of Applied Behavior Analysis, 7,* 271–285.

Brooks, B. D. (1974). Contingency contracts with truants. *The Personnel and Guidance Journal, 52,* 316–320.

Campbell, M. (1981). *Teaching contract negotiation to parents of adolescents.* Unpublished master's thesis, University of Kansas, Lawrence.

Cantrell, R. P., Cantrell, M. L., Huddleston, C. M., & Woolridge, R. L. (1969). Contingency contracting with school problems. *Journal of Applied Behavior Analysis, 2,* 215–220.

Hall, R. V., & Hall, M. L. (1998a). *How to select reinforcers.* Austin, TX: PRO-ED.

Hall, R. V., & Hall, M. L. (1998b). *How to use planned ignoring (extinction).* Austin, TX: PRO-ED.

Hall, R. V., & Hall, M. L. (1998c). *How to use systematic attention and approval.* Austin, TX: PRO-ED.

Hall, R. V., & Hall, M. L. (1998d). *How to use time-out.* Austin, Texas: PRO-ED.

Homme, L. (1969). *How to use contingency contracting in the classroom.* Champaign, IL: Research Press.

Kazdin, A. E. (1994). *Behavior modification in applied settings.* Pacific Grove, CA: Brooks/Cole.

Kelly, M. L., & Stokes, T. F. (1982). Contingency contracting with disadvantaged youths: Improving classroom performance. *Journal of Applied Behavior Analysis, 15,* 447–454.

Long, J. D., & Frye, V. H. (1977). *Making it till Friday.* Princeton, NJ: Princeton Book.

Mann, R. A. (1972). The behavior-therapeutic use of contingency contracting to control an adult behavior problem: Weight control. *Journal of Applied Behavior Analysis, 5,* 99–109.

Miller, D. L., & Kelly, M. L. (1994). The use of goal setting and contingency contracting for improving children's homework performance. *Journal of Applied Behavior Analysis, 27,* 73–84.

Panyan, M. (1980). *How to use shaping.* Lawrence, KS: H & H Enterprises.

Sulzer, E. S. (1962). Research frontier: Reinforcement and the therapeutic contract. *Journal of Counseling Psychology, 9,* 271–276.

Sulzer-Azeroff, B., & Mayer, G. R. (1991). *Behavior analysis for lasting change.* Fort Worth, TX: Holt, Rinehart and Winston.

Van Houten, R. (1998). *How to motivate others through feedback.* Austin, TX: PRO-ED.

Weathers, L., & Liberman, R. P. (1975). Contingency contracting with families of delinquent adolescents. *Behavior Therapy, 6,* 356–366.

Wysocki, T., Hall, G., Iwata, B., & Riordan, M. (1979). Behavioral management of exercise: Contracting for aerobic points. *Journal of Applied Behavior Analysis, 12,* 55–64.

Notes

Notes

Notes